The Rising

THE RISING

Awaken, Heal, Inspire

By Ashley A. Barnes, MS

Copyright © 2018 Ashley A. Barnes, MS

True Bliss Publishing
Louisville, KY

ISBN: 978-0-578-41931-2

Printed in the United States of America.

The Rising

Awaken, Heal, Inspire

by

Ashley A. Barnes, MS

Contents

Rest now in peace, dear Mother
For the light of love has pierced the darkness And
hope shines on the horizon

Introduction

"Our deepest fear is not that we are inadequate. Our deepest fear is that we are powerful beyond measure. It is our light, not our darkness that most frightens us. We ask ourselves, Who am I to be brilliant, gorgeous, talented, fabulous? Actually, who are you not to be? You are a child of God. Your playing small does not serve the world. There is nothing enlightened about shrinking so that other people won't feel insecure around you. We are all meant to shine, as children do. We were born to make manifest the glory of God that is within us. It's not just in some of us; it's in everyone. And as we let our own light shine, we unconsciously give other people permission to do the same. As we are liberated from our own fear, our presence automatically liberates others."

~ Marianne Williamson,
A Return to Love: Reflections on the
Principles of A Course in Miracles

I remember when I first read this quote. It was in 2011, and I was just starting my health coaching study program. It was included in our packet of materials for clients, intended as a tool to motivate and encourage. It did much more than that. It was the start of my liberation from fear and the recognition of my light. The awakening to my gifts as an energetically sensitive, intuitive healer and writer. The ongoing work of healing from my mother's death and a multitude of seemingly bad choices and wrong turns, which ultimately led me to the person I am and the work

I do today. And the overwhelming pull (and endless pushing from my angels) to stop staying behind the scenes and realize that my gifts, my passion, and my leadership are needed to make a difference in the world. It was the catalyst for my Rising, facilitated through the process of awakening, healing, and inspiration. It is my sincere hope that this book is that catalyst for you.

The poems collected here are for you, especially if you are experiencing a newfound opening inside which calls for deeper meaning and purpose, a growing desire to do something more in a world where chaos and darkness seem to grow stronger by the day. As an art form, poetry is a powerful medium during personal and collective crises, giving an inspirational voice to moments of gravity when few other genres can suffice and often moving us to take inspired, collective action. Likewise, the poetry in *The Rising* invites you to do just that – to connect to and draw from your inner power –the light within – and use this to create more of the same in the world, using three distinct yet interconnected stages as your guide: *Awaken, Heal,* and *Inspire.*

In Awaken, you will explore the need to not only come to terms with the immense suffering of people all across the globe, but also with your own suffering, as well as your own bright light. In doing so, you will find you are more able to embrace your innate gifts and use them to be the change so needed in this time of upheaval. Once awakened, you will discover in Heal that your conscious choice to transcend the pain of your past and heal your suffering is at once a blessing, a curse, and your greatest gift to the world. By healing yourself, you inspire and give others permission to follow your lead. In the final section, Inspire, you will cement your vision for yourself and become motivated to rise up as an inspirational leader for yourself and for our world.

The steps seem simple, yet are not necessarily easy to accomplish. They require deep work, a willingness to be open in a world that doesn't always value vulnerability, and the courage to stand tall when others shrink around you. Though many forms of activism call for us to harness anger and pain in order to make change, your way of "fighting" may appear more peaceful: writing, art, prayer, intuitive or healing work, acts of service, or simply taking the first tentative steps to heal. Regardless of how you are led to show up, the world needs you to awaken to the suffering in others, the planet, and in yourself. To take steps to heal that which tethers you to the wounds of the past so you can more effectively be the change for the future. To turn your intentions outward that you may use your gifts and experiences to inspire and be inspired. The world needs YOUR gifts, YOUR passion, YOUR leadership.

The time is now, the time is here, to rise up – in your truth, your own perfect imperfection, and in your burning desire to awaken, heal, and inspire *The Rising*.

Part 1

Awaken

To the realities of this world,
Though painful, we cannot turn away;
Too many suffer, ourselves included,
Yet continue to turn a blind eye;
When we open to the realities of others,
When we open to the gifts set before us,
We can see and use these gifts,
To see the change,
Be the change.

Eyes for Truth

In the green
In the mean
Great hearts insist
Persist
Their path is the only way
Here we stay
Longing
Belonging
For another way
All lives precious
Their worth unseen
If only we had eyes for truth
And warring hearts made clean

Unlimited Soul

A thousand years from now
Can we even imagine
That humans will still exist,
Our reign on this earth
Still tearing from the lifeblood
Of our fellow man and beast,
All creatures crying for the day
When justice will end the tyranny?

Or will the sun set on sickness and lack,
As we rise with the full moon
Above the utopia of our dreams,
Straight out of the mind,
Through the sci-fi writer's pen?

It's hard to imagine the collective
Moving any way at all these days,
The seemingly infinite reaping
Of mistakes gone past
Without regard for future's coming,

The infinity of man
Only a keyhole guarantee
For the unlimited soul

Angels Weep

Not one of us is free
Until all of us are free

We hide behind our laws
Our badges
Our guns
Our politics
Our fears

We hide behind
What we have convinced our hearts to believe
About those with whom we share this earth
Yet our souls know the truth

That all people bear the light inside
While only some wear the chains of inequity
Only some taste what they believe is real freedom
And even they are often fooled

For power does not equal freedom
Nor does an unholy clinging to the idea
That only some are worthy

Not one of us is free
Until all of us are free

And the angels weep

Prayer for Peace

Oh God,
This prayer for peace
Falls faintly from the lips of man,
Eroded by the deeds of doers past,
Shrouded by their heavy hearts

Clinging to belief in hope instead of action,
Fighting to bring peace,
Loving only those
With whom we can agree,

Our doctrines, temples, broken hearts
Could not prepare us for this time,
All built on rocky layers
Of prejudice and doubt,

And so we dig from beneath the rubble
Of our own unsteady hearts
To salvage what humanity we have left,
To create the second coming,
A new world within

Do You Feel It Too?

I feel a restlessness growing,
A deep inner knowing,
The power rising up,
My hands like a cup,
Overflowing
Fear, it is retreating
Our wings, lightly beating
Do you feel it too?

Caged Animal

The ties that bind
And constrict,
Contort,
Tether us to the past
Like caged animals
Fighting to be free,

Until no amount of fight is left
And we succumb
To the numb,
The resolute acceptance
That pain is our legacy,

And yet,
The cage walls are soft and fleshy,
Ready to be transgressed
With a gentle touch of love and softness,
A gentle asking for release

War is not the way,
Only peace begets the peace
Our animal craves,
And only with peace
Do we know how to be free

The World that Is to Come

Our shared humanity
Comes crashing down
With one evil deed,
The love we share, shattered,
Never to return to innocence

Yet true love –
Soul love –
Cannot be broken,
True connection does not end
With the sniper's fire

Connected as one we rise,
Our ashes sealed together
From our creation,
Fused in light,
Experienced together in flesh,
Forever as one

Emanating from Source
Rays of perfection
In an imperfect world,
Rising as we can,
Setting as we must,
Each day a new challenge

To not lose hope,
Not sway from faith,
But rather draw strength from inside
For the world that is to come,
Created within,
An eternity in the making

New Wave Coming

There's a new wave coming,
In our hearts we feel the swell,
The aching, anxious pull
To rise up

Open throat and heart
To speak the words unspoken,
To right the wrongs unchallenged,
To wield the sword of grace
While taking no more dark lies
Festering in the hearts of men,
Their poison oozing from every pore

Yet this wave will cleanse us all,
Pounding over us without pity,
Bringing each man to his knees
In anger, anguish, and shame,
Hearts finally open,
Eyes finally capable
Of seeing each other,
Just as we are

A new wave on the shore
The entire ocean in a drop

What If You Knew?

What if your life
Could transform the world?

What if we told you
Your very existence
Could ease the living
Of beings you've never met
And never will?

What if you chose
To live your life in a way
Which does no conscious harm,
Yet intuitively sets out
To be the example,
Not of perfection,
But of perseverance?

What if you knew
You already carry this light,
Deep within,
That you already have the power,
For with each breath you take
You make a difference?

What if you knew
That you were living it already
Simply by striving
To always be you?

Spirit Calling

Do you hear the voices calling,
Calling, calling?

Can you feel their spirits falling,
Falling, falling?

For the connection with their love is fleeting,
Fleeting, fleeting;

And the time has come to be meeting,
Meeting, meeting

Calling, falling,
Fleeting, meeting
This time is ours to rise

Rising, rising in resistance
Crying, crying with persistence

Our time is now
Our peace is now
Spirit calls us now

Be, Do, Love

What date will be stamped
On your heart
As the day when you knew,
When you could no longer run
Or hide,
Or pretend in the waking up
That you are still the same,
That your ever-breaking heart
Cannot go on in its pretense,
Insisting that it's too weak
Yet knowing the depths
Of its strength,
Knowing that the day has come,
The time is now
To be, do, love
All that you ever dreamed,
All that you ever have been
All along

Can You Feel It?

There is change coming
can you feel it in the air?

Do you feel it wrapped around you
like a blanket,
the cold stickiness like a hard-earned sweat?

Do you feel the palpitations
like a heartbeat,
the life-blood of your dream?

Does it keep you awake
imagining all that is to be,
all you are to become?

Do you feel it in your bones,
calcified to the truth
in the great grey matter,
a living scheme of color?

Do you feel the change,
and what, my friend,
will you do to make it happen?

Let It Rise

When the fire in your belly burns hot
Let it rise
Let it burn up the untouched debris of your heart
Let it cut the cords of inequity
Which still tie you to your waking grave

Burn the ashes of your untouched past
The parts you thought were shattered and lost
Still piercing the hidden portals of your heart

Melt each smoldering layer
Until only the truest you remains
No longer fighting for life
But shining eternal in your own pure light

Peace is Possible

The day of reckoning will come,
The day for all arms
To be placed upon the ground,
Rendered unusable by the peace which pervades,
Which dulls the blades
And melts the bullets into molds,
Rendering new weapons in its stead

A new execution of harmony in our time,
Enforced not with violence
But with handcuffs of love,
Locked together, embracing
This timeless truth:

Peace is possible
War is not inevitable
Love is not an illusion

But rather each are tangibles
Which we give freely,
Lifting us from the torment of fear
Rising, rising, to the peak
Where peace speaks
And love, it reigns eternal

I Am Open

Fill me with your words. I am open.

Sing me the song of the Universe, that it may escape my lips for all the world to know the tune, even if they can't find the words.

Fill me with the stories of ancients, that I might know the destiny of man and speak the message to all who hear.

Fill me with the glory and the power of the Christ, let me know the sacrifice, the vision of Heaven on earth, Hell in our own hearts, the rising of Love.

I am open to your voices. Your song resonates in my heart.

Purge the emptiness, fill it with your kingdom, the vibration of oneness.

Mold me, shape me in the ways you will have me best exist in this world as a conduit of love.

I am open.

New World

The time has come –
Once a whisper, now a battle cry
A wail in the deep soul of man;
The time for change,
A shift from fear to love,
To the lifeblood which fuels not one
But all

No longer can fear sustain
Or right the ways
Perpetrated for centuries and lifetimes,
Pain carried like a cross
Beating down on each next generation;
These days have past
And love has reared its pink-hued head,
A tipping point on the brink
And the tides are turning

Chaos embroiled with daily living
The disorder of change in our eyes
The sand in the glass raining down
On those who will not transcend
Swallowed whole, yet not before
Taking down with them incidental passersby,

Their stillness an easy target,
Those who stake a flag may fall as well
Yet their sacrifice paves the way
For me and you

Where do you fall?
Where do you land?
In this new world,
Where do you stand?
In this new world order,
Everyone must make a choice
Complacency can no longer rule the day
Nor fear obstruct our way

A Warrior for Your Own Heart

The well's dried up
Its water a mere trickle,
A puddle,
Muddy and unmoving
And a voice whispers,

"You must seek another source.
You're plugging the wellspring
With your own self-doubts
And the muddied energy of the world.
No wonder you have no flow.

You must dive in headfirst
Without fear or delay,
Find where the water ceases to fill you any longer,
No matter the time or breath it takes.
Your drowning in the process
Won't be in vain
For you will rise up stronger,
More divine than ever before.

Dive in to rock bottom,
Seek your source,
Re-emerge, a warrior for your own heart."

One Love

The world sits in wary wonder
And wonders, what will we do?

The world sits in silent sadness
And wonders, what will we say?

The world sits in persistent pain
And wonders, what will we change?

The world sits and looks to us,
And we look inside
At our wariness,
Our sadness,
Our pain,
And we wonder, what can we do,
What can we say,
What can we change,
As one life,
One heart

The world reaches for our hand
And whispers,
One step,
One word,
One love,

You've got this.

This Is the Day

This is the day it all changes
The day you take your life
In your own hands, throw off
The connections that have
Held you back
This is the day
You open your heart to love

Crack open all the forbidden places,
Protected by fortresses of dust,
Locked away after the hurt
That could not be tolerated, the pain
That sealed the final lock and consumed
The key

This is the day that you swim
Into the belly of the great fish, find the way
Of salvation and go shaking into the depths
To release your soul, no longer a prisoner
Of your own making

The wind may howl, wild and raging storms
May attempt to block your path,
But the fallen branches in your way,

The uprooted trees that shake your foundation
Are no match for you,

Your heart is strong and your whole life
Has brought you to this moment

This is the day.

Part 2

Heal

Once awakened to our own suffering,
We must do the work that sets us free,
Not only for ourselves,
But for the world,
For each step taken in grace towards the light
Opens space for another,
And another
Until we all are healing,
Creating a ripple, a high tide,
Washing away the pain
So that it no longer rules us,
But instead guides us
To the next steps of our healing,
And the healing of the world.

Alive

People are alive,
Exploding from nothingness
Into awakening of senses,
Angry, restless, urging to step out
Make their presence known in this changing world

Where do we fit in?

How do we carry the light of justice and truth
Without getting burned in our own flame?

The sign of backlash is inevitable
In a world so full of passion,
So full of hunger for a new existence
Truth no longer gets use hanged or drowned,
Yet it still takes years sometimes to set us free

And so that freedom we seek
Must come from within,
Chains may hold our bodies
But nothing except lies and fear
May constrain the soul

Feel It Now

Time's up
It's over
The opportunity
Is no more

For those who refuse to see
The light within their hearts,
To feel the goodness of their souls
And the souls of fellow men,

To experience the river running through,
Connecting each of us to one another,
Swift waters carving a clear channel
As they deftly move on through

No, the time is now
For those who look away
To miss out on their great gifts
And for those who participate
To seize the day

Not in victory,
But in love,
In the power that only connection
To Source energy can bring

Feel it now
Coursing through
Feel it now
Cleansing you

For the Love of All

The light of life has come,
And with it, no time to run
Or hide our faces in shame
Any longer,
For the light seeks out those
Who own their transgressions
And stand for truth,
Who recognize the past
Is simply past,
Who make amends and choose
To step forward,
Again and again,
Into the night,
Carrying the light,
Creating a new way,
A new day,
Light for the life,
The love,
Of all

Am I the One?

In the laughter
And the tears,
The loving and the hating,
The anger and the joys –
Where do I fit in?

Do I shrink like a violet,
Or rage like the stormy sea,
Should I wrap myself in gold dust,
Like a star,
And go shooting across the sky?

Does my great open heart
Need to be contained,
Or can I laugh my way across
The galaxy within my soul?

Does no one know?
Does no one hear?

Or am I the one not listening,
Not speaking the words I live,
Confused by laughter,
Driven by hate?

Am I the one who twisted fate,
Am I the one who through my love,
Can make things right again?

Lift You Up

I carry the weight of a hurting world this night
All the sadness, all the pain that man can muster
And these wings feel too tattered to lift me up,
Lift me up

Deep within, I know this is not mine to carry
Yet this weight bears down,
This torch I willingly choose, this is who I am, at once
a burden and gift,
Tonight this light shines dimly only on the feet just
below me,
On my own broken path

No matter how much I will through words
Your suffering be transcended
Angels, gods, bended knees, and clasped hands
Can't stop your deepest hurt
It finds you in the darkest places
Where you try so hard to keep out the light

Even the caress of these weary wings
Won't make you whole
The mosaic of your tears, burning up the night
But if only for an instant, may they lift you up
Lift you up

Shield of Love

We run through life
Deftly avoiding all the trip-ups along the way
The stones that mar the path,
The crevices that catch an ankle,
Giving the illusion of speed,
In actuality more like the turtle,
Hiding in her shell

Little turtle, held tightly
Within the safety of her hardened refuge
Refusing to acknowledge the light of day
Yet shells can crack and break,
And she whispers to me:

"Do you know what I have given up?
For this safety, I traded darkness
And am forever alone,
The world runs on by past me
In its hurry to avoid,
Not so different from me, I dare think."

And she whispers too, as I run away,
"It's time to stop the running now
Take off the armor of avoidance

Carry the shield of the warrior,
The fighting is near,
And no amount of running and hiding
Can stop it

Only eyes to see,
An open heart,
And a shield of love"

What If?

What if the only way to be free
Is to give up all we've ever known
To turn our backs on that which
Has painfully brought us to this place
All the lies we brought inside
And raised like bitter children
Never letting them see the light of day
For fear their faces would be too much to bear

All the stories told late at night
Embedded in our minds
Like handprints in fresh concrete
First told when only the wind howled in our empty souls
Hands cold from clutching at a heart
Already too far down the path to be constrained

What if we had to admit
That it was all a fallacy,
That grief can't keep us grounded
And fear won't make us whole,
That it's only in receiving
That we're able to give,
And it's only in faith
That our hearts open to love?

Phoenix

The bleeding starts
And runs right through,
Piercing all the hearts,
Staining the very clothes
That kept it out of sight
And silent in the world
Where it so violently wanted sight
And to be seen

And so she opened up the wound,
Made it visible to those who once turned away,
And striking a pose of resistance,
Cried her faithful tears
Until the bleeding had to stop,

And in its place,
And from her death
The great red bird rose and flew,
Freedom on its wings,
All she ever wanted,
All her bloody heart ever knew

A World Worth Saving

And there you spend your waking days
rising like the sun in the east
setting right all the painful wrongs
that ever crossed the lips of man

There you cross the valley
lighting up the shadows
that were once so carelessly tossed aside
by evil, hidden from the light of man

And there you lie down,
let the waves wash over you,
the sand bury your bones
until you rise up again,
as every drop, as every sea
you rise up as the bearer of wings
that drop their feathers like hope
to the ground, a blanket of healing dreams
for a world worth saving

Become the Way

Rising energy
Of the setting sun
Isn't lost on heavy hearts,
The winds of change howling in our ears
Instead, the pressure lifts us up,
Rising to the peak of our existence
Where we see blue above the clouds,
Sun on the horizon
From another side of the world

This perspective gives us wings
To raise our fearful energy to grace,
Envelope our hearts in compassion
For a darkened world turned light
And lift our healing hearts into the sky,
Rising, rising to meet the sun
The light, merging and emerging,
Into night, into day
Become the way,
For a people led astray

Freedom Found

In the shallows
Of my sun-swept heart
The light finds its way
Into the spaces only meant
For lovers and mothers,
Into the gray-depths
Which conceal the hidden treasures
Of the soul

Longing, seeking,
Calling out to be free,
Yet engaging with the tender truth
That freedom surely isn't free,
That to be truly uncensored
Means another must be bound

And so, standing fully in the light
The soul knows,
The soul sings of freedom found
Only in being bound
Each soul unto all others

Gathering of the Flame

This light, so hard to carry
This light, so difficult to bear

At times, more a burden than a blessing
More a challenge than an easy road

And yet our hearts still call us to the flame
As moths endure their sacred dance

To fly despite the burning
Strip down the wings but not the character

Nor the pollination of beauty,
Keeping light alive

Even with burnt wings
Even when hope seems futile

The gathering of the flame
Is our birthright and our quest

Set You Free

I've sat in darkened hallways
Head between my knees
As silent tears echoed to the floor
I was there when you cried too

I've sat beside the bedside
Held the withered hand
As life slowly crept out of its shell
I sat there at the bedside with you too

I've sat beside the ocean
Words and waves lapping at my feet
As new worlds opened up inside
I sat beside you as you opened too

I see colors inside you
I feel new life emerging
In the quiet of the morning
I hear words only your heart can sing

The light it grows inside you
Each day it longs more to be free
So familiar, yet so foreign
I sit beside you, set you free

Live It Now

Time stands still
And in the void an otherworldly voice
Begins to whisper from some unknown depths within,

And though her language is unknown
The heart still understands
And begins to whisper too

Softly at first, then growing louder
Until the voice becomes a roar
For all ears to receive:

It is not by the color of our skin
Or the hairs on our heads,
The sound of the voice in our throats
The pew in which we sit,
Or the love we hold in our hearts for another
That we are persecuted so,

No, it is the brokenness,
A carried-down, ancestral aching,
Fierce clinging to ancient, entrenched philosophies,
Hunger misguided by survival of the fittest
Which tortures and feeds our collective broken heart,

The weeping dagger still twisting
In the open wound
Never bearing the opportunity
To experience the light of healing

Those who hold the power to turn the knife
And keep the wound always fresh and weeping
Believe they also hold the key to our survival
Yet they are wrong,
They mask a heart-known truth

We also hold the handle to the knife
And turn its blade deep into our own flesh
Each time we choose hate or indifference over love
Each time we choose personal safety over protection for
another
Each time we choose blindness rather than witness a
painful truth
Each time we choose, repeatedly, not to remove the knife
From our own bleeding hearts

And so when we choose to fight the knife-bearers
Without removing our own blades,
We also then choose
To fight ourselves

This truth, it lies inside each one of us;
To heal the world, to heal ourselves
We must speak it now,
We must live it NOW

What the World Needs

The world needs to hear your peace
To see your actions of gentleness
And love
The world needs you to be strong and soft
In your heart
Not powering through
But loving full out
The anger
The trauma
The pain
The world needs you broken open
And willing to serve
The world needs your big heart

In These Times

In these times
Of war, chaos, hate,
In times where people seem
As if they cannot come together,
They will not be as one

Even those with similar beliefs
Still keep their walls of difference
Close by

Times when people in the streets,
Those who cry in their hearts for change,
Those who quietly accept
Or loudly sound the battle cry
From behind closed doors and bright screens
Are the criminals

In these times
When troubles weigh heavy
And escape seems a better route,
We have a place of refuge
In candlelit spaces
Somber and still

We find our voice,
We connect to our strength,
We discover the power to resist armies
And soothe even the most lost and frightened soul

There they call us by name,
Sing out for all time:
The song of our souls,
The light of our hearts;
Directing us on the path
Through the darkness of these times

A Light for the World

The seat of the soul lies buried deep;
It's time to let it out,
Dig it up and share it with the world
The time for fear is past

This life is different,
It holds a power greater than any before
The power of change,
The power of love,
Stronger, more attainable than ever

The world may think us mad for claiming to see it,
The scorched earth before us belying all the senses
But we know it,
It's in our bones, our DNA,
In the particles which create us from the inside out
We know it because it lives in us,
Breathes in us
It longs to be free of us,
To reside in the world as us

We can no longer ignore, in fear and distrust,
What we know in our bones to be true,
For it is in us, it IS us
And we are a light for the world

New World Rising

The light of day
Brings new hope and inner stirrings
As our outer shells crack open,
Hearts longing to reveal
Newly-formed skin into the world,
Exposing vulnerable flesh
Still oozing from new birth

We stand,
Ready and radiant in our new forms,
Gowns glowing gold and sparkling in the early light,
Moving through the fog of hope and confusion,
Forging a path through the wilderness of our existence,
Taming golden light into a new awakening

Drawing in the darkness,
Breathing out the love of ancients
Into a world rising from its own ashes

Love, Heal, Reveal

It's in our blood,
Our greatest depths of being
To love, heal, reveal

To give the world
The love only we can
To heal the wounds
Of generations before us
To reveal the light
Each of us carries inside

To love ourselves
As no other can
To heal ourselves
As no other will
To reveal ourselves
So that we may be
Made manifest by the light

The love is now
The healing is now
The revealing is now
Go forth and carry the torch,
So that others may have a path in the fog,
Fumbling through the darkness,

So that others may tread more simply,
Creating a new world

Loving
Healing
Revealing

Part 3

Inspire

And then we seek to inspire
Both ourselves and others,
As we awaken and the healing layers fall away,
We carry our newfound light into the world
In the ways only we know how
The only limitation our own imagination
For we are unique souls
On a mission,
With a vision,
Uncovered through our awakening,
Our healing,
Brought to life through inspiration,
To become leaders of the light

The Light of Your Own Existence

When the time is right, you'll know it—
The trumpet sounds in your ear
Your heart light shines brighter than ever
The whispering angel who guides you
Will not let you forget

Through all the madness and destruction
You may hope to ignore the signs that await you
Yet a chorus of light still calls you to your higher purpose,
Your soul guides you home

Not down the safest path, but through the thorny brambles,
Risking life and limb and all you've known
To serve the light inside

The fear is often great, and many falter
But not you—
For you are the transmuter of fear,
The one for whom you have waited,
The light of your own existence

The Time is Now

The time is now
The time is here,
When all the angel voices cheer

Rise up, rise up
And take your heed,
Time to serve a world in need

The time is now
When we all speak,
Rise up and be the one you seek

For in this day
And in this age,
The rising starts with all our rage

And rises up
Into a song,
A message that we all belong

Voices of Angels

Forward thinkers always looking backwards,
Collecting all the news of yesterday,
Using it to build their empires,
Walls to keep some men out and others
Tucked safely behind false dichotomies

What is this world where the thinkers close their minds,
Make themselves scarce while the rest decay?
What is this world where the bravest of those are put down,
Shunned, or locked away?

When did we stop hearing the voices of angels,
Or trusting that our truth would guide us home?
When did we stop listening?

Though don't despair, for while many throw bricks
At glass houses hoping for change,
There are those who seek to advance the light
While maintaining the shadows on themselves,
Who walk in utter darkness
So others may know the joy of love's light on their faces

We may not think we know them,
Though we most likely do,
We simply don't have eyes open yet to see

Yet we can listen with our hearts,
Listen for the tender mourning of a world
Ready to go home

Leaders of the Light

The days march by
slowly at first, then picking up speed
until one day there you are
picking up the pieces
of a life you never wanted
how did I even get here, you ask
But you know.
That mindless clock kept ticking
and you kept marching
and well here you are
pondering your divinity
on top of the mountain
called Responsibility
and Loneliness
and as the wind blows
cold against your defeated tears
a familiar voice whispers,

"It's not too late."

And the chill that passes through
your tired body
the hairs that stand on end

like a forest at attention
that is how you know

The thumping of your heart
the lump in your throat
it's enough for you to at least consider
to stop the marching
dismantle the mountain
reroute your path to the present
attract more presence for the future
know that you are light incarnate
share that light from your high vantage point

For we can all be leaders of the light

Inner Space

In the great here and now
Everything's changing
Everyone's turning
Eyes to a new light

Some with hope and devastation
Some with the light of new life
Each fueled by the desire
For inner peace and love

The changing ones are leading
In the back doors of our minds
With carefully planted words and songs

Right up front in the conference halls
On the screens
In the churches
On the scenes

Yet pay attention to the quiet ones,
The ones who lead with gentleness and service
In the backdrop of the crowd

For Jesus even said, "Blessed are the meek"
And the meekest of us all
May possess the inner space
To hold the love that opens up
All our starving hearts

The Spark

Blue skies and sunshine
can't conceal the hollow
emptiness that remains,
at times the tragedy
is too much,
no amount of rainbows
can color life better,
all around, the world moves
people move
but you, immobile,
vortex spinning 'round,
paralyzed by indecision,
you are the answer
to all your fears,
your single movement
the start of our great change,
your fleeting thought, detained,
the spark that sets man free

The Time When Light Won

If at first
You don't reach the light
Try, try again,
For the light is not found fleeting,
Yet we are,
Our thoughts lost
In insincere and meandering ways,
Victims of the chaos that surrounds
With no preference to whom it takes asunder
In the throes of life

And so, we must not give up hope
Or lose ourselves to fear,
No matter how justified,
For these are the days of fortitude
And progress through transgression,
These are the days when we will recall
To our children's children
The time when Light won

Shining Light of Peace

Where can we make the most change,
Where can we shine the brightest light,
Who needs it most?

In the dark,
In the long night of the soul,
Who needs what we have to offer,
In our humbleness,
In our mystery,
The light shines within,
A gift to those all around,
Those whose paths
Lie directly in ours.

Who are we to shy away,
To hide our light in fear and shame,
Who are we to avoid the calling,
To be our best,
Shine our brightest,
Not only because the world needs us,
But because we need ourselves

To rise up,
In the night,
A shining light of peace for all

Keeping Hope Alive

Do you hear the bells ring?
Do you hear the children sing?
Keeping hope alive

In the dark night of transition
When change electrifies our hearts
How do you keep hope alive?

The days march on in untimed cadence
With the songs of fighting in our hearts
Hope no longer seems alive

Deep inside the whispers grow, become a mighty roar
Reverberating through our very nature
We are the ones who keep hope alive

Forward moving, never stalling, reaching out a hand
Shining light in this dark land
Keeping hope alive

Be in Love Together

Keep churning out those words
That love, a gift for a people
Who don't even know
What they need,
Lacking in love
Yet too blind to see

So we fight
And we hate
And we strive to protect our own
Not realizing our own is me
And you,
Each other in this together

No one gets out alive
But we can be in Love
Together

Visioning

What's the vision of the future?
The one we see in dreams,
Details silently appearing, one-by-one,
As we paint the pictures of our lives,
Following the path to paradise,
Long and winding, the end unclear

Yet we feel compelled to keep on moving,
Keep on building,
Keep on visioning
Until the future comes fully into sight,
Created from our own dedication,
Our determination,
Our courage to persevere

For the good of man and beast,
For our very own existence,
The call inside too deep to ignore,
The vision too real to let go

Today I Choose

Today I choose Life

I choose Freedom

I choose raw vulnerability

I choose the Road Less Traveled

I choose Courage and Honesty

I choose to reach deep inside

To the depths of my humanity

And become what I already am

You Are the Prayer

You are the prayer
Quietly whispered by the Creator
In the moment you were breathed into existence
The spark which lit the night
And sent awareness into the skies

You are the prayer
Silently held in the lonely chapel
Beads tightly gripped in sweaty hands
Hoping for a god of miracles

You are the prayer
The joyous celebration of songs sung
From the high cathedrals of the heart
Echoing through the halls of your soul

You are the prayer
Of the grasses and trees
The flowers, the streams, the wind, and the bee
You are the last hope, the savior
The one who wields the power to harvest the future

You are the prayer, the song
The sanctuary of the collective soul
You are the one you've been waiting for

We All Are Now Home

Making our way, on down the line
Through the cadence and chorus, the withering vine
Of time on the lam, down lanes in the rain
Flitting like butterflies, wings stretched to the sun
Ready and waiting, new adventures to come

Despite flashes of lightening, rumbling across the great sky
The path we are travailing, a dark stain in heart's eye
Full of the perils of a life fully-lived
Dodging the arrows so generously given

Piercing our hearts, allowing the bleed
To drain us of that which we don't really need
Leaving a path for others who follow
So their way may be easier, less difficult to swallow

Forsaking ourselves for the task at our hand
Marching along to our very own band
The sun setting lower, the time drawing near
Undaunted by difficulty, hard work, or fear

The time is at hand, the time where we know
The new world is upon us, we all are now home

The Connection Between Darkness and Light

Time to rise up,
Face the day,
Become the warrior you're meant to be,
Become the solider in the trenches
Facing off with the darkness,
Residing in the hearts of man,
Fighting your own darkness first,
Not to eradicate
But to reveal,
To illuminate,
To make whole again
The connection between darkness and light
For one cannot exist without the other
Yet both must be visible
For balance to be achieved,
For wholeness to be experienced,
For equality to be had by all

The Rising

In the great mosaic of our lives
There comes a time
When the calling becomes a trumpet in our ears,
And the will to lay down arms in love
Is stronger than the will to fight,
When the rising stirs inside,
And might no longer makes right

But rather we rise up
To awaken in the sleeping world,
And do the work that must be done
To heal our cracked and bleeding souls,
Mend our hearts and forge the bridges
So our love may inspire a movement,
And the light may shine on through,
As the great rising inside becomes an anthem,
A love song for all the ages

In the rising, we find peace.
In the rising, we connect to love.
In the rising, we take action to make our lives what we
know in our souls they can be.
In the rising we awaken, we heal, and we inspire.
For ourselves. For all beings. For a world worth saving.
In the rising, we are One.

How Do You Help
the World?

You LOVE~
    Love yourself
    Love your neighbor
    Love your enemy
    Love the less fortunate
    Love the fortunate
    Love the dictators
    Love the soldiers
    Love the hateful
    Love the animals
    (all of them, even the very tiny)
    Love the plants and trees and water
    Did I mention to love yourself?

Love with the heart of the Creator
    the spirit of the angels
    the precision of the universe within your soul

I Am

I am
The light in the darkness
The one I seek to drag me up
Soothe my soul
Embittered by the wounds of youth

I am
The power for which I yearn
The strength to overcome and start anew
To right the wrongs of a past
Lustful for drama and pain

I am
The lens through which
You see my soul
Today bitter, tomorrow emboldened
A flash of greatness a thousand lifetimes in the making

I am

About The Author

Ashley Barnes, MS, is a poet and author of two books, *The Angel Inside: Inspiration to Connect with Your Inner Guidance* and *The Rising,* as well as her active blog of "Poetic Healing" and the "Daily Bliss" angel messages. Ashley rediscovered her passion for writing nearly fifteen years after losing her mother to a long battle with cancer, using poetry as an outlet for healing, exploration, and discovery of her own deeper connection to her inner guidance and spiritual gifts.

As a writer, her true love and gift is the written word. As such, she writes for empathic women who are waking up to their true selves and feel guided to make a greater impact in the world through a commitment to self-healing. In addition to writing, Ashley is a certified coach and Reiki Master/Teacher who leads women's circles, workshops, private healing sessions, and holds space for the Facebook community *Awakening Angels Women's Circle.* She is a board member of Woman to Woman Kentuckiana, a non-profit committed to women's empowerment, and also enjoys a ten-plus-year career in leadership and organizational development, where she has the privilege to facilitate the growth of individuals while also funding her creative work.

She's happily married with four children, a granddaughter, and too many pets to mention, which helps to satisfy her undying love for animals of all kinds. She lives in "Kentuckiana"

USA; however, her heart is always in the magical sand and glorious green water of Siesta Key Beach, where she feels most inspired and at home.

If you want to learn more about Ashley's work, purchase a book, read the Daily Bliss, and to learn when new releases come out, visit her website at http://www.aspiritledlife.org, where you can sign up to receive email updates and inspiration.

CPSIA information can be obtained
at www.ICGtesting.com
Printed in the USA
FFHW020848021218
49718865-54136FF

9 780578 419312